First printing 2021

Published by
Lioness Pride Visions Publishing
www.LionessPrideVisions.com

admin@ezzylane.com

ISBN: 978-0-578-83297-5

Printed in the United States of America
10 9 8 7 6 5 4 3 2 1

To get the full effect of this book, please open your camera on your device (phone, tablet, the camera on computer).

When the QR code has been read by your camera, click the link, and choose your platform to stream the song of your choice. You can also click the link here: www.hyperurl.co/ColorWheelEzzy

Enjoy your fun musical experience!

-Ezzy Lane

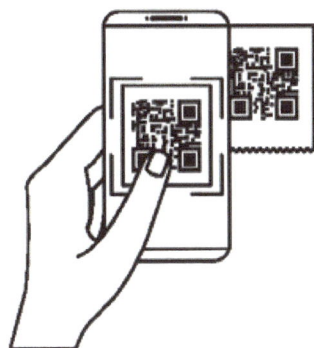

Dedication

I dedicate this book to every child in the world that loves to learn through music.

Sang by:
Ezzy Lane

Welcome To The Color Wheel Experience!

Vol. 1

Yours Truly,

Enzy Lane

It's the Color Wheel
Yeah, yeah, yeah Color wheel
It's the color wheel yeah, yeah, yeah
Color Wheel
RED, YELLOW, BLUE
RED, RED, YELLOW, BLUE
RED, YELLOW, BLUE
RED, RED YELLOW, BLUE
It's the Color Wheel
Yeah, yeah, yeah Color wheel
It's the color wheel yeah, yeah, yeah
Color Wheel
RED, YELLOW, BLUE
RED, RED, YELLOW, BLUE
RED, YELLOW, BLUE
RED, RED, YELLOW, BLUE

RED

Cherries, strawberries
Stop signs and fire hydrants.
Rudolph the reindeer's nose is the brightest.
The color of my blood when it hits the air.
The same color as this Coca Cola can in my hand.

Red Red Red Red

Red   Red

Red Red Red Red

Just like the sky, the sky high.
The color of 2/3rd's of the earth, oh my.
Some berries, some fish, the planet Neptune.
When I'm not feeling well, they say I look ...
BLUE

Blue   Blue   Blue   Blue

Blue   Blue

Blue   Blue   Blue

Blue   Blue   Blue

YELLOW

Like the lemons freshly squeezed.

Under the summer sun when it's 90 degrees, now that's hot.

The bright dividing lines in the streets.

Or the caution signs that say be careful when I cross the street

Now.

Can you mix a color to get RED?
NO
Can you mix another color to get BLUE?
NO
Can you mix two colors to get YELLOW?
NO
These are primary colors but there's something you can do!

It's the Color Wheel
Yeah, yeah, yeah Color wheel
It's the color wheel yeah, yeah, yeah
Color Wheel

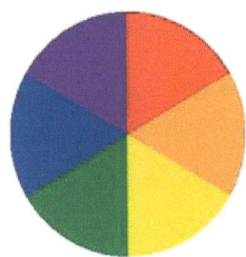

RED, YELLOW, BLUE
RED, RED, YELLOW, BLUE
RED, YELLOW, BLUE
RED, RED, YELLOW, BLUE

It's the Color Wheel
Yeah, yeah, yeah Color wheel
It's the color wheel yeah, yeah, yeah
Color Wheel

RED, YELLOW, BLUE
RED, RED, YELLOW, BLUE
RED, YELLOW, BLUE
RED, RED, YELLOW, BLUE

Take some YELLOW,
And add a little RED.
What do you get?
ORANGE
A color that we know is fun.
A juicy fruit that we squeeze and American cheese.

Now, take some BLUE and mix it with some YELLOW.
What do you get?
GREEN
The color of the GREEN grass and the leaves.
The frogs in the pond.
They jump on lily pads.
Make sure you eat your broccoli when it's done.

Entwine BLUE & RED and you get
PURPLE.
All african queens wear this on their royal garments.
Eggplants, violets
Remember Barney loves you!
Don't forget the plums.
And those sweet sweet grapes, too.

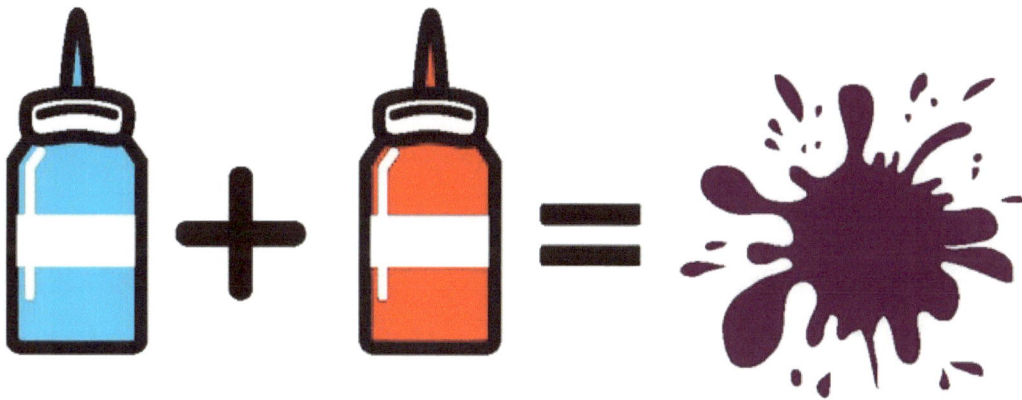

We mixed two colors to get ORANGE.
Then we mixed two colors to get GREEN.
So we mixed two colors to get PURPLE.
Those are secondary colors.
I knew you'd know what I mean.

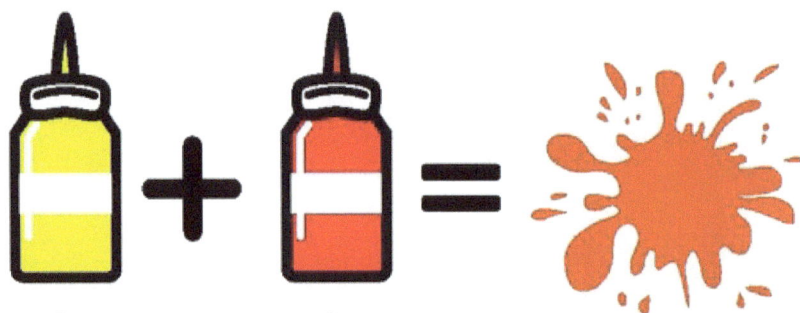

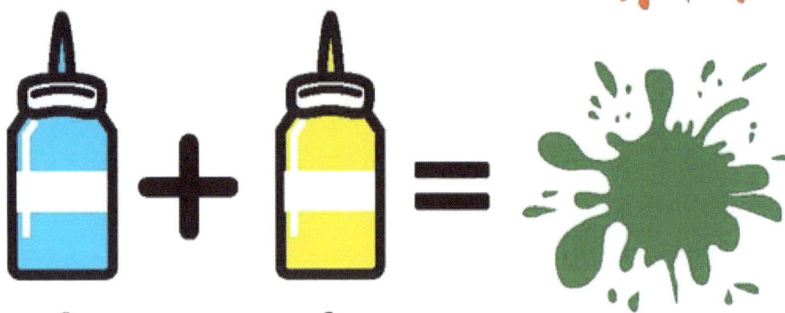

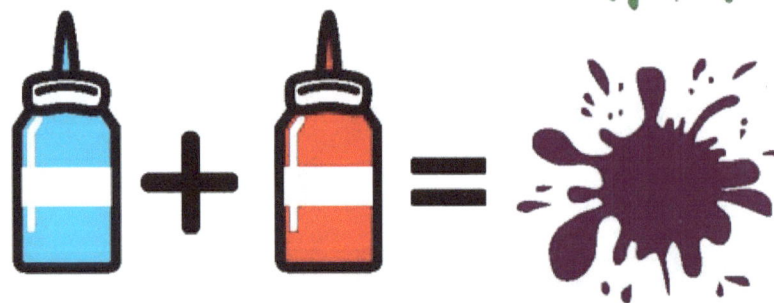

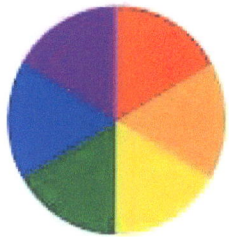

It's the Color Wheel
Yeah, yeah, yeah Color wheel
It's the color wheel yeah, yeah, yeah Color Wheel
RED, YELLOW, BLUE
RED, RED, YELLOW, BLUE
RED, YELLOW, BLUE
RED, RED, YELLOW, BLUE
It's the Color Wheel
Yeah, yeah, yeah Color wheel
It's the color wheel yeah, yeah, yeah Color Wheel
RED, YELLOW, BLUE
RED, RED, YELLOW, BLUE
RED, YELLOW, BLUE
RED, RED, YELLOW, BLUE
Yeah, yeah, yeah
Yeah, yeah, yeah
Yeah, yeah, yeah
Yeah, yeah, yeah
RED
BLUE
YELLOW

It's the Color Wheel
Yeah, yeah, yeah
Color wheel
It's the color wheel yeah, yeah, yeah
Color Wheel
RED, YELLOW, BLUE
RED, RED, YELLOW, BLUE
RED, YELLOW, BLUE
RED, RED, YELLOW, BLUE

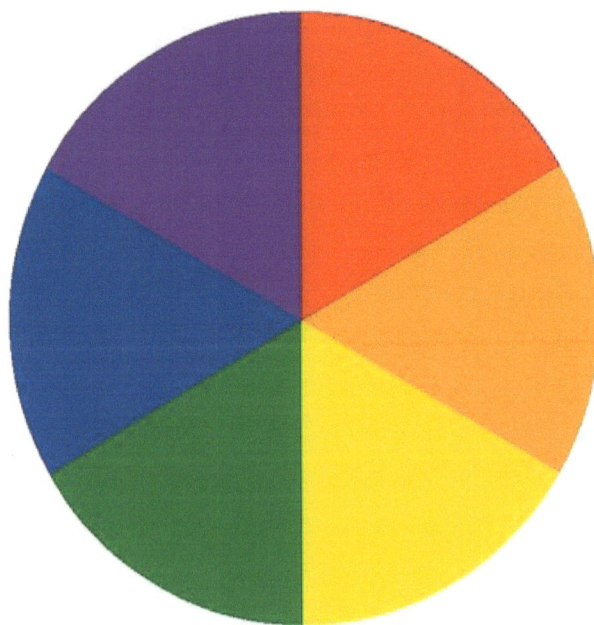

Yeah, yeah, yeah
Yeah, yeah, yeah
Yeah, yeah, yeah
Yeah, yeah, yeah

www.ingramcontent.com/pod-product-compliance
Lightning Source LLC
Chambersburg PA
CBHW041244040426
42445CB00004B/138